essentials

Writing Successful Essays

Time-saving books that teach specific skills to busy people, focusing on what really matters; the things that make a difference – the *essentials*. Other books in the series include:

Selling Your Home Using Feng Shui

Writing Good Reports

Speaking in Public

Responding to Stress

Succeeding at Interviews

Solving Problems

Hiring People

Getting Started on the Internet

Writing Great Copy

Making the Best Man's Speech

Making Great Presentations

Making the Most of Your Time

For full details please send for a free copy of the latest catalogue. See back cover for address.

The things that really matter about

Writing Successful Essays

Brendan Hennessy

ESSENTIALS

Published in 2000 by
How To Books Ltd, 3 Newtec Place,
Magdalen Road, Oxford OX4 1RE, United Kingdom
Tel: (01865) 793806   Fax: (01865) 248780
email: info@howtobooks.co.uk
www.howtobooks.co.uk

British Library Cataloguing in Publication Data.
A catalogue record for this book is available from
the British Library.

Edited by Diana Brueton
Cover design by Shireen Nathoo Designs
Cover copy by Sallyann Sheridan
Produced for How To Books by Deer Park Productions
Typeset by Anneset, Weston-super-Mare, Somerset
Printed and bound by Hillman Printers, Frome, Somerset

NOTE: The material contained in this book is set out in good faith for
general guidance and no liability can be accepted for loss or expense
incurred as a result of relying in particular circumstances on
statements made in the book. Laws and regulations are complex and
liable to change, and readers should check the current position with
the relevant authorities before making personal arrangements.

ESSENTIALS *is an imprint of*
How To Books

Contents

Illustrations

*Mind Map® is the registered trade mark of the Buzan Organisation

Preface

Since the essential guidance for essay writing doesn't change from one level to another, I believe this book will benefit students from age 14 to MA level, with A-level the average pitch of the text. I have very much kept in mind the needs of mature students who have returned to formal studies after a period away from them, and students from overseas. Anyone in working life, who has to produce pieces of writing (from advertisements to business reports) that require basic planning and writing-up skills, should also find the book useful.

Essay writing can become a chore if you plunge in without clear objectives. It can become a joy, however, if you know how to select a topic that will keep you enthused, prepare well and master the other basic skills. Practise what this book proposes, and you will find increasing satisfaction with your essays, and the motivation to improve with each one.

A note on style. 'Quote' is used for extracts from speeches or ordinary texts, 'quotations' for classic literary quotes.

I am indebted to the following organisations for permission to reproduce essay titles: ULEAC (University of London Examinations and Assessment Council), the Open University, Oxford Delegacy of Local Examinations and the Southern Examining Group.

Brendan Hennessy

1 Embracing Your Topic

*Commit yourself wholeheartedly
to producing what the topic requires.*

5 things that
really matter

1 UNDERSTANDING WHAT THE TOPIC REQUIRES
2 GETTING THE QUESTION CLEAR
3 INTERPRETING KEY TERMS AND INSTRUCTIONS
4 PARAPHRASING THE TOPIC
5 CHOOSING THE TOPIC TO LIVE WITH

It is rarely a good idea to start writing an essay without giving the topic some thought. Most pieces of writing involve common activities: **formulating ideas**; **deciding on purpose and audience**; **deciding on content, structure and style**; **planning**, **collecting information** and **note-taking**; and **making a draft or two** before writing the final version.

We start with the five things that really matter in the process of thinking about essay topics offered and of choosing the one you feel you can **do justice to**. 'Doing justice to' is not simply a matter of which topic you like most, or which topic you feel you know most about. Ask yourself if you are tempted to choose such topics because you feel you know most of the answers already or because you feel it will be easier to write about. Another topic might induce you to collect information more diligently. The result might be a more original essay that would satisfy better a tutor's or exam board's expectations.

IS THIS YOU?

● *I'm trying to get started on an essay entitled 'How does Celie's character change from oppressed teenager to independent woman through* The Colour Purple?' *'How does it change' – what does that mean? It's changing all the time. It's all about poor blacks in the southern United States at the turn of the century. She's physically and sexually abused, and raped by stepfather and husband, finds somebody to love, her self-esteem grows, she starts a business . . . but so many things happen – where do you start? I've got pages and pages of notes but I don't know what to do with them.*

 ## UNDERSTANDING WHAT THE TOPIC REQUIRES

The question on *The Colour Purple* is apparently quite straightforward. But **even the simplest question needs to be interpreted**. The student faced with this essay hasn't appreciated that '**how** does it change' means: **illustrate** the changes, that is, **explain with examples.**

The most common fault in essays is failure to answer the question. Read through the topics and be clear about their requirements before making a choice.

The student is right to say that Celie is constantly developing throughout the novel, but what is needed are her **crisis points**. These are where there's a crucial change – a significant stage in her development. With this understanding, the student would have made much fewer but more relevant notes. Having identified Celie's crisis points, the student needs to explain **who** and **what** help her develop at each point.

Other topics, especially at GCSE level, are expressed as

neat titles, without either instructional words or question. Supply instructional words when they are missing.

Consider, for example, 'My last birthday'. This topic is **creative**, and it seems to leave you free to choose your content. Assume the missing instruction is **describe** or **give your memories of**. But beware. Your tutor will expect you to show some **imagination and writing skill**. Don't merely recount the main events of the day in chronological order or narrate events that could have happened on any ordinary day. Because it is a creative essay you would be expected to reflect on the significance of the birthday in your life, humorous perhaps if not weighty.

Evoke your memories as vividly as possible. Bring to life the people who gathered round you on that day, and describe any noteworthy incident in an interesting, perhaps dramatic, way.

Other, more complex topics need to be interpreted very carefully. Take, for example: 'Argue the case against the banning of corporal punishment of children in schools'. If you're strongly against corporal punishment, you may be delighted to find that term in an offered topic. Here it would be easy to leap in and answer the wrong question: to argue the case **against** corporal punishment. But the two negatives **against/banning** cancel each other out. Together they make a positive. The topic, in fact, requires you to argue **for** corporal punishment.

 GETTING THE QUESTION CLEAR

Take care with three categories of topic:

- Where there is an implicit question, not expressed.

- Where the topic requires several sentences, or is built round a quote or quotation.

- Where there are underlying assumptions, which need to be recognised.

The following topic fits these three categories: 'People don't seem to realise that it takes time and effort and preparation to think. Statesmen are too busy making speeches to think.' Bertrand Russell. Discuss with reference to *either* Winston Churchill, the war leader, *or* Clement Attlee.

Clearly there is some truth in the quoted statement but it is not the whole truth. If you don't unravel the question behind the instruction **discuss**, the danger is that you may think you have been asked to find only evidence that supports the quote, ignoring the other side of the argument.

One way of dealing with a topic that contains a question that has not been expressed is to **turn the statement into a question**. In this case the question would be something like: 'How accurately do you think Russell's statement applies to the career of. . .?'

You should question the assumptions of a topic.

In this case the quote used as a basis for discussion need not be taken at face value. Isn't the **way** a statesman thinks, you might want to argue, as valid a way of thinking as the more philosophical kind? But an essay in history, not philosophy, is wanted. Here you could indicate your reservations about the quoted statement but go on to apply it as required.

INTERPRETING KEY TERMS AND INSTRUCTIONS

After reacting to topics as a whole, you need to look at elements more closely. They are of three kinds:

1. **Key terms or concepts.** These indicate what area of subject matter your essay should cover.

2. **Instructional words.** These tell you what to do with the subject-matter. Explain, argue, discuss and so on.

3. **Other pointers** to what is expected include such phrases as 'how far', 'in what ways'.

Before rushing into your essay, identify the key terms in your topic – underline them. **Key terms need to be defined.** For example: 'Argue the case against the <u>banning</u> of <u>corporal punishment</u> of <u>children</u> in <u>schools.</u>'

● **Banning**, in such a general context, may be defined as prohibited, made illegal.

● **Corporal punishment** needs more care. There is a wide range of corporal punishment, from a slap on the wrist to grievous bodily harm, and you will have to decide where you draw the line.

● **Children.** Then you realise it depends what you mean by children. How will the definition of 'corporal punishment' vary according to different ages of children? Should the criteria, moreover, be the same for parent, nanny, child-minder and teacher?

● **Schools.** Are you to consider primary, secondary, special needs?

You can see that by analysing the key terms of the topic in this way you may be formulating a **basic outline** for the essay.

The meanings of key terms can also vary according to context and subjects.

> Use your dictionary, of course, to help you define key terms, but note how much meanings can vary according to context. For example, consider how you would define 'banning' in this context: 'Do you agree to parents banning television until homework is completed?'

Meanings can also vary according to subjects or disciplines.

> For most topics **poverty** will have a straightforward meaning, but for an essay in sociology you might have to take account of various definitions of the term employed by different theorists. You might have to indicate where they disagree, and where you stand.
>
> If writing a literature essay based on a quotation, be careful to identify where a key term carries a contemporary meaning different from its current meaning. If you are asked to discuss, for example, Hamlet's 'Thus conscience does make cowards of us all' you will need to be aware that 'conscience' carries the meaning of 'knowledge' or 'awareness', not its current meaning.
>
> It is also important to make sure you **interpret the instructions correctly**. The following is a list of instructional words that students occasionally misinterpret:

> **compare** find similarities and differences between
>
> **contrast** indicate the differences between
>
> **discuss** examine in detail, argue, give reasons for and against
>
> **describe** give a detailed account of

illustrate	explain with examples
refute	prove a statement/argument to be false.

 PARAPHRASING THE TOPIC

When you find it difficult to get your head round a topic, try putting it into your own words: **paraphrasing it**. Let's do this with 'Argue the case against the banning of corporal punishment of children in schools'. It could be paraphrased as: 'What are the arguments for keeping it legal to give corporal punishment to children in schools?'

It's always advisable to check your paraphrase with your tutor or a fellow-student: if it's incorrect, your essay will go off the rails. Suppose you came up with the following effort at paraphrase: 'Do you think corporal punishment in schools should be made illegal?' Your resulting essay might express your views clearly and persuasively. Unfortunately, it's **one side of the argument** that is required, not (except incidentally) **your views**.

 CHOOSING THE TOPIC TO LIVE WITH

The title of this chapter uses the word **embracing** to emphasise **the need for commitment** to the topic you choose for a term essay. You must feel that your chosen topic will allow you to do justice to the abilities you possess, which the essay has been designed to test. In general terms, essays test that you can:

● collect information quickly and use the knowledge to focus clearly on the set topic

● read critically and purposefully

● analyse processes and problems and argue a case

- relate theory to specific examples

- make a creative (original) contribution to the subject

- structure the material logically, express it clearly and present it in the format expected.

There may also be specific requirements for your essay, which your tutor will advise you of.

Embracing a topic means keeping it constantly in view.

If you don't keep a topic constantly in view you will waste time studying and noting the irrelevant, and you will digress when writing up. You can keep it in view by:

- putting the title on a card and displaying it above or on your desk.

- writing the title as a heading to your work at every stage – notes, plan, first draft, final version.

MAKING WHAT MATTERS WORK FOR YOU

(After completing these exercises, check with the Responses in Appendix A, page 59.)

1. 'My last birthday' lacked an instructional word and we supplied 'describe' or 'give your memories of'. Add a short sentence or two to the following titles in order to suggest how they should be treated:
    (a) 'My favourite restaurant'
    (b) 'If I were Prime Minister'
    (c) 'Friendship'

2. Turn the following topic into a question: 'Refute the arguments that are made in favour of caring for the mentally ill in the community'.

3. Underline the key terms in the following topics:
    (a) 'Wisdom is wasted on the old'. How far do you agree with this statement? (The 'creative' type, more likely to be set at GCSE-level.)
    (b) Why were Allied Forces able to make rapid progress in their North African campaigns during 1942–3 but slow to make progress in their Italian campaigns of 1943–5? (GCSE Modern World History, June 1993, ULEAC.)
    (c) Does the increasing popularity of fringe religious groups indicate that secularisation is a myth? (A-level Sociology, May 1983, Oxford.)

4. Paraphrase each of the topics of exercise 3, supplying suitable instructional terms where not stated.

2 Taking Notes

A good note-taking system will help you to produce accurate and relevant information from the start.

5

things that
really matter

1 **WORKING TO A TIMETABLE**

2 **NOTING IDEAS**

3 **NOTING FACTS AND OPINIONS**

4 **ORDERING YOUR NOTES**

5 **PARAPHRASING, SUMMARISING AND RECALLING**

Avoid taking too many notes, which will make it hard to see a pattern to follow. Avoid taking too few: you may run out of ideas half way through the writing. Take the right amount of notes by **keeping their purposes** constantly in mind.

The three purposes of note-taking are:

- **To stimulate your own thinking** on the subject so that there is some originality in your viewpoint or argument. At all stages of note-taking, jot down your own reactions.

- **To collect information accurately**, in the form of ideas, opinions and facts. Check one source against another, depending on the time available.

- **To collect relevant information**. Take a little more than you need, and select the most useful. Relate your research to the topic you are covering by writing the topic at the head of all sections of notes, drafts, etc.

IS THIS YOU?

● *I'm not very good at taking notes at class lectures and I miss important points. If I borrow a friend's notes afterwards I can't read their writing or I can't decipher their system of abbreviation or I can't work out their thought processes. Once I start reading the necessary books or articles I become so fascinated by the subject I read much more than I need to, following all the interesting byways of the subject, and I take far too many notes. I then have a terrible job selecting what is relevant and putting it in order. I am generally late submitting my assignments.*

 ### WORKING TO A TIMETABLE

A short essay (say up to 500 words on 'The street I live in') may be written out of your head and may need only one draft. Any topic requiring greater length and complexity has to be done in stages. **Make a timetable**, working back from delivery deadline, showing when you should complete:

● notes of your immediate reactions to the topic

● survey of the sources of information suggested (course outline, reading lists, companies/individuals to interview)

● research of your subject area and topic

● one or two essay plans

● first draft

● final version.

NOTING IDEAS

Aim for some originality from the start. Consider the topic: 'Do you think that ageism among employers in this country is on the increase?' Here is a useful plan of action:

- Note what ideas you already have on the topic.

- Test your own ideas against those of others.

- Stimulate your thinking by brainstorming.

The simplest brainstorming method is formulating some of the questions that an analysis of the topic provides. One question will suggest another.

Examples

1   What are the typical manifestations of ageism? A general lack of attention to elderly people's ideas, feeling they are out of date? A suspicion that their faculties have been much diminished, or are fast diminishing?

2   In which parts of the country is there more evidence of ageism?

3   At what age do people typically find barriers to employment on the grounds of age?

4   In what kinds of employment is ageism most prevalent? Lower-paid work? Middle management level? The professions?

5   What recourse to the law do victims of ageism have? How effective are the safeguards? Is the control over ageist adverts effective? (Talk to Age Concern.)

Initial ideas can be put into the form of a **mind map**®, in question or statement form, especially if you have quite a lot of ideas in your head at the start and you want to look at them and play about with them immediately. A mind map used at the planning stage is illustrated on page 21. You now know what you are looking for and can begin to research your topic at greater depth. The essential research skills are as follows.

③ NOTING FACTS AND OPINIONS

Know how to use a library. Get to know a reference library intimately and use it regularly, including the computerised databases. Acquaint yourself with the indexes that list articles published in newspapers and magazines, and with directories that list details of organisations (such as Age Concern) that would supply you with literature about subjects you are studying (such as ageism) and may agree to be interviewed. The librarian will always help.

If you use the Internet there may be a gateway site that will help you to select relevant and reliable information.

Sample books to judge their usefulness. Note for example the qualifications of the author, the date of publication, the contents page and main headings, the index and the preface to judge how relevant to your topic the book is.

Read books at the level they demand: skim, scan or read in depth. Skimming means quickly exploring the ground, noting what will be useful for your purposes. **Scanning** means that you search out exactly what you want, ignoring the rest. **In depth** means that you read the relevant parts, questioning critically.

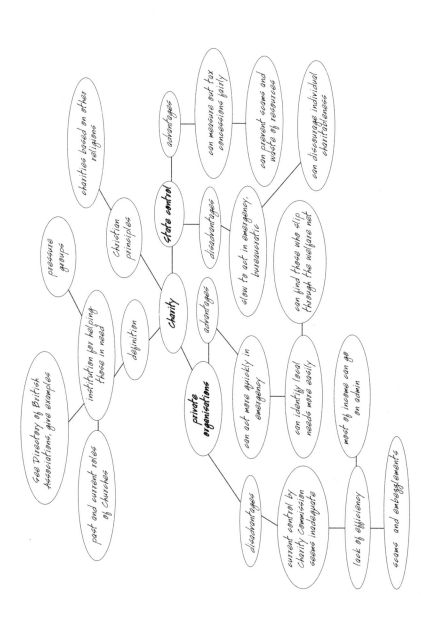

Fig. 1. Mind map® for an essay on 'Should charity be left to the state'?

To back up your viewpoint, you are just as interested in opinions for evidence as in facts. But it is authoritative opinions that you are interested in: that is, opinions based on facts.

Strongly based views may be based on lack of knowledge or misunderstandings. An elderly interviewee, for instance, may believe that he was turned down for a new post on the grounds of age. Further research may reveal that the company decided to distribute the new tasks among existing posts rather than create a new post.

Your supportive material will be enlivened by **anecdotal evidence**, that is stories and case studies, and by **illustrative examples** and **analogies** that make your discussion clear.

Indicate the sources for your notes. At the writing up stage you may need to refer back to the sources to check that you have noted them accurately, or to quote from them, indicating how far you agree with them. It is a good idea to put your own reactions to what you are noting in square brackets [ ] as you go, so that you can easily see at writing up stage where you stand, and the pattern that your discussion is likely to take.

Do not assume that any fact is correct, however renowned the author, or that any opinion is valid, however authoritative, or that any anecdote has been remembered clearly. Many errors creep into books and newspapers. Check one source against the other when there is doubt, and you have the time to do so.

In practice you will be expected to base your discussion on a balance of reasonable evidence. You will save time by carefully selecting reliable sources from the start.

ORDERING YOUR NOTES

Use whichever arrangement or combination of arrangements suit you best for particular projects. Make sure you indicate sources and prepare a separate **bibliography** if you refer to several books and articles. Recommended arrangements are:

- a simple folder

- a loose-leaf ring binder

- note cards

You may want to combine one or two systems.

A simple folder. For an essay up to 1,000 words a simple folder may be sufficient, to contain perhaps lecture notes, notes from a book or two, and from a few articles, and photocopied newspaper cuttings and leaflets with the main points highlighted. You may also have pencilled notes in books of your own (not to be done in library books). Ideally, select the most relevant notes and transfer them to A4 sheets, with a new sheet for each aspect of your topic, writing on one side of the paper only.

A loose-leaf ring binder. For lengthier projects requiring more notes and materials. Use dividers to separate different aspects.

6" x 4" note cards. They can easily be ordered by shuffling. Cards encourage you to be concise and to paraphrase rather than copy slavishly.

5" x 3" bibliography cards. Shuffle them into alphabetical order as you go, and you have an ordered bibliography to copy at the finish. Cards are illustrated on page 24.

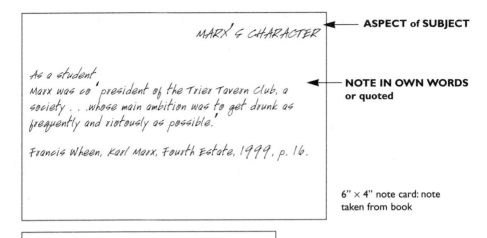

MARX'S CHARACTER ◀——— **ASPECT of SUBJECT**

As a student
Marx was co-'president of the Trier Tavern Club, a
society . . .whose main ambition was to get drunk as
frequently and riotously as possible.'

Francis Wheen, Karl Marx, Fourth Estate, 1999, p. 16.

◀——— **NOTE IN OWN WORDS**
or quoted

6" × 4" note card: note
taken from book

COMMUNISM

Wheen, Francis, Karl Marx, Fourth Estate,
1999.

Shows Marx to have been an unstable
character with little to say about a future
communist policy, though intellectually gifted.

5" × 3" Bibliography card:
book's value noted

Fig. 2.   Note cards

 PARAPHRASING, SUMMARISING AND RECALLING
Take notes in your own words. Paraphrasing will ensure
that you will end up with an original approach to the
subject and not merely a re-hash of others' views, without
any ideas of your own. Passages used as evidence must be
enclosed within quotes. There should not be too many
quoted passages and they must be integrated into your
essay by having their relevance to the topic commented on.

Summarise to avoid taking too many notes. As with
paraphrasing, you are using your own words and putting
your own stamp on the material.

Use an abbreviation system: eg, 'Prepg essay, gd note
takg systm = accte relt info.

Oral recall. Get a fellow-student to question you on your notes or texts. Note any lapses in your responses.

Written recall. Study any important section of your notes or texts, put it aside and write a summary of the main points. Then check.

Review. Read through all your notes, checking against the texts for accuracy, filling in any observable gaps.

MAKING WHAT MATTERS WORK FOR YOU

You are writing an essay about organic food and need to make a brief reference to the increased demand. Note two important points as far as possible in your own words (not more than 20 words for each point) from this extract from the article 'Planet Organic' (*The Observer Magazine*, 27 June 1999). Assume that the information is up to date.

Anyone who has stepped into a supermarket recently will be aware of the explosion in demand for organic food. Waitrose and Sainsbury's now stock more than 400 organic lines, and their rivals are making strenuous efforts to catch up, while organic restaurants, cafés, juice bars and greengrocers are springing up in urban high streets. At the moment, 70 per cent of organic produce is being imported: domestic farmers and growers can't keep up with demand, although, for the first time in history, more land is now in conversion (a process that takes about three years) than in production, and the Soil Association reckons that it receives 40 calls a day from farmers eager to make the switch.

3 Finding the Best Plan

*Planning helps you to think fruitfully,
to discover what you want to say and
how to put it into a coherent shape.*

3

things that
really matter

1 **USING BRAINSTORMING TECHNIQUES**

2 **SELECTING THE CONTROLLING IDEA**

3 **MATCHING PLAN TO TOPIC**

Thoughts, as they come to us, are rarely in coherent order. Listen to a conversation or even a tape-recorded interview and the best of thinkers ramble and repeat themselves. You may, nevertheless, find that you think more fruitfully in the act of writing. You like to jot down a few main points and dive into a rough draft, leaving the re-ordering and planning until later. For most essays, however, you will need to impose order at an early stage by planning.

There are two kinds of plan:

- **brainstorming**, generally a creative, informal kind

- **linear-logical**, or **formal**.

Experiment to discover the kind of planning that best suits you and your topic. We start with the informal kind, because it is especially useful at the early, idea-forming stage. It can be used at any later stage too, when you are at an impasse.

IS THIS YOU?

*In an essay on pizza restaurants I stated categorically that Pizza Express was better than Pizza Hut. I thought the crusts were thinner and the toppings thicker. Also Pizza Express is more up-market and my friends seem to prefer it. My tutor said I was begging the question: assuming to be true what I was supposed to be proving. Did upmarket necessarily mean better? She showed me a recent report in **Which?** that contained a survey of pizza restaurants, showing that on most counts Pizza Hut won more points. We can't talk about conclusive proof in such matters, my tutor said, but a survey using many people from a wide range, asking many specific questions, is much more reliable evidence than I had gathered. The opinions were more **informed**, clearly based on facts. She guessed rightly that I had not planned. 'If you had, you would have done more thinking and produced some useful points.'*

USING BRAINSTORMING TECHNIQUES

Brainstorming means **experimenting with word and idea associations**. The various techniques help you to discover fresh ideas. We have seen the simplest technique in operation: formulating questions and letting one question (or answer) suggest another (see page 19). Here are other brainstorming techniques:

- The five WS plus how.

- People and Perspectives.

- Mind Maps®.

Five Ws plus how. Newspaper reporters are programmed to collect evidence by asking who, what, where, when, why and how? The essay writer can often work in the same way. Let's associate those questions with a topic and see how we would group the evidence. 'What is the evidence that suggests that watching too much television can be damaging?'

- Who: affecting whom – young child, college student, housewife or househusband?

- What: dangers of increasing passivity, of reducing attention span, of killing conversation.

- Where: TV sets in different rooms of a house.

- When: How many hours of the day?

- Why: arguments, for example, based on the way television tends to provide answers rather than ask questions.

- How: TV watching becomes addictive, unselective, 'chewing gum for the eyes'.

History, politics and sociology essays benefit from this approach.

Some topics are best served by a version of the above technique, called **People and Perspectives**. Confronted with 'Why did Henry II quarrel with Thomas Becket, Archbishop of Canterbury?' you may be full of facts but unable to see a path through them. The order of the names implies that the perspective of the king is wanted. Clearly the **attitude** of the king to Becket's defending the rights of the Church against those of the monarchy needs to be covered. The psychological facts as well as the constitutional facts are needed. One you've studied the period, put yourself into the king's place and imagine how he felt about

Becket. You can now see a way of ordering and shaping your ideas.

If you have time, you may want to read a play about Becket, for example T.S. Eliot's *Murder in the Cathedral* or a more recent one, and set its theme alongside the historical facts.

Mind Maps®. The main advantage of mind maps (also called mind webs, concept trees and 'spiders') is that they encourage lateral thinking. This means thinking sideways, illogically, unpredictably, with the aim of finding fresh approaches and ideas for a topic. Study the mind map on page 21 for the topic 'Should Charity be left to the State?' You follow one aspect out from the middle of a page. Then because you can see them all at once, as you see a landscape from an aeroplane, you see other connections sideways that you wouldn't see with a logical scheme, which is more like seeing the landscape from a train.

 SELECTING THE CONTROLLING IDEA

A controlling idea is needed to give an essay unity and coherence. That idea, depending on the topic, might be more appropriately called a viewpoint, a thesis, a theme or an explanation.

You may find it hard to write without a plan. Or you may find the more interesting ideas come to you in the course of writing.

A short essay will have a controlling idea imposed early on (prisons should be fewer/ fewer people should be imprisoned/ more prisons should be built).

If you find a controlling idea soon after researching, you will find it easier to avoid digressing and taking too many notes.

Keep in mind the **basic outline**:

- **introduction**, or beginning

- **body**, or middle

- **conclusion**, or ending.

 MATCHING PLAN TO TOPIC

There are simple and detailed versions of the logical plan. The simple version is **building points into paragraphs**. A straightforwardly narrative or decriptive essay requiring little exposition or argument can be planned with a list of points.

Take, for example 'My local leisure centre'. The points might be: the building and its setting, the layout indicating the various facilities, the pool or pools, the various facilities at the pools (diving boards, chutes, waves, etc), other attractions for children, facilities for other sports (gymnasium, squash, etc), sauna, cafeteria or restaurant.

Five hundred words might be divided as: 60 words for an introductory paragraph, 40 words for the conclusion, and about 50 words for each of the eight paragraphs of the body.

The points may be expressed in a **statement-per-paragraph plan**, a particularly useful form for a simple argument such as: 'Parents should bear more responsibility for the crimes of their children'.

For an essay largely in agreement with the proposition the statements would no doubt include:

- The quality of parental guidance seems to be deteriorating.

- But punishing parents (eg by fining) only destabilises the family further.

- Schools have to bear too much of the blame.

- The police cannot be expected to do more monitoring of young delinquents.

At an earlier stage of a project, or for an essay that is going to be less sure of its position, the points may be arranged in a **question-per-paragraph plan**:

- Is the quality of parental guidance deteriorating? . . . and so on.

For longer projects, where the notes are fairly numerous, a **detailed formal plan** will be most convenient. An example with some linking indicated, is given in Appendix B.

Test your plan before writing up:

1. Is there a unified theme?

2. Is every point relevant and well connected

3. Do the title, introduction and conclusion chime, as a team, making it clear what the viewpoint is?

MAKING WHAT MATTERS WORK FOR YOU

✓ Make a question-per-paragraph plan for the topic 'What may be the effects of an increase in leisure time?' (GCSE Sociology, June 1993, ULEAC.)

4 Beginning and Ending

Begin with a promise that attracts interest. End by showing that you have fulfilled your promise.

5 things that really matter

1 **INTRODUCING WITH A PROMISE**

2 **AROUSING INTEREST AND CURIOSITY**

3 **SUMMING UP AT THE END**

4 **FINALISING THE QUESTION**

5 **LEAVING SOMETHING TO THINK ABOUT**

The beginning (introduction) and ending (conclusion) add up to **about a third of the essay.** The ending is usually a little shorter than the beginning.

They are usually the most difficult parts to write, but attempt them in the first draft to keep yourself on track. Rewrite them after the body is done, when you realise what you have actually said.

Much can be learnt from studying the beginnings and endings of newspaper features and magazine articles. Broadsheet ones are closer to the academic essay and don't tend to sacrifice substance to style or entertainment, as the tabloid features can. Tabloid features, however, can teach us a lot about how to attract attention.

Fulfilling the promise of an essay means **establishing your viewpoint.** You will have explained or argued with conviction, and you will have persuaded the reader at least to think about what you had to say.

IS THIS YOU?

I tend to write boring beginnings and endings. The beginnings explain what the title means and what I am aiming to do. They are usually clear, but I don't seem to be able to make them readable. Then, although the body of the essay may be well structured I don't see how to round it off. I feel I've covered the ground so that there's no more left to say. The essay comes to a sudden stop, and it reads as though I've run out of ideas.

① INTRODUCING WITH A PROMISE

The beginning, or introduction, has to be a link between the title and the essay. It must indicate, either explicitly or implicitly:

- what the topic means

- how you intend to limit the subject.

The start of an essay by Graham Greene, the novelist, called 'The Lost Childhood', does these things subtly and concisely:

> Perhaps it is only in childhood that books have any deep influence on our lives. In later life we admire, we are entertained, we may modify some views we already hold, but we are more likely to find in books merely a confirmation of what is in our minds already: as in a love affair it is our own features that we see reflected flatteringly back.

Where the viewpoint is more tentative, or the topic is complex, as in 'Is the work ethic outdated?', the writer may choose to take the reader by the hand and give a slightly more detailed idea of the plan to be followed. It might run like this:

I shall show how the work ethic has developed through history . . . its association with (as examples) Christian and Muslim principles . . . compare the force of the work ethic in present-day Christian and Muslim states . . . the role of government . . . the role of the media . . .

When you signpost the order of well-defined sections in this way you must of course **keep to that order in the body of the essay**. You will have made it easier for yourself to make the transitions from one section to the next: the reader is anticipating you. The reader will not prefer the essay to have had more impact, more liveliness, if it would have been at the expense of clarity.

Clarity is the most essential quality of an essay.

 ## AROUSING INTEREST AND CURIOSITY

Whether you are indicating viewpoint or signposting what is to come, aim to **arouse interest** at the same time. It will sharpen attention for what you have to say. Ways of arousing interest are:

1. **Move from abstract to concrete**. You could begin an essay by saying that during the Second World War airmen came into a hospital badly injured. Or you could immediately make it concrete, to let the reader see it. You could, for example, tell an anecdote or relate a startling fact or statistic. An article in *The Mail on Sunday* begins:

There were four ways in which airmen used to come into Ward 3 of the Queen Victoria Hospital in East Grinstead during the war: boiled, mashed, fried and roast. "Just like potatoes really", said one of them.

2. **Use a quotation or a quote**. A student's essay on 'What is education for?' begins:

> I think the 19th century philosopher Herbert Spencer expressed it best, certainly most concisely. He said, "Education has for its object the formation of character" . . . I believe its purpose is, or should be, to help us to develop the character and skills to live at peace and earn our living in the society we find ourselves in. I believe the key quality to acquire for this is balance

Note that in a subtle way the student is both defining the key term 'character' and updating the associations.

There are numerous books of quotations, from both classical and modern authors. Make sure the quotation you choose is **relevant**, and no more than one (at the most two) per essay is advised in general. Essays on literature, of course, may demand many quotations and often quotes (eg, from critics, commentators) as well.

What is said in a quote is usually more important than **who** said it. Experts will be quoted to add authority. Celebrities are often used for quotes in newspapers because they are a convenient shorthand for getting across the context. Writing about ageism, an article in *Ms London* magazine begins:

> 'You can be a 50-year-old anything except a 50-year-old actress,' Faye Dunaway said recently with some bitterness. In truth, ageism is a form of discrimination that doesn't only affect thespians and doesn't only affect 50-year-olds. Age discrimination in employment can affect everyone.

Notice how briskly the relevance of the quote is established by the viewpoint.

3. **Make the reader laugh or cry.** The quote about the airmen is enough to make you cry. Humour or wit is a wonderful way of making a point memorable if you can avoid relating a joke for its own sake because you believe it's a good one rather than for its appropriateness to your theme. There are books of humorous quotations; you can ransack the great humorists of the past for yourself; you can note how it's done in weeklies such as *Private Eye* and *The Spectator*, and in newspapers and magazines that print humorous essays and personal columns and you can be funny on your own account.

 SUMMING UP AT THE END

Summing up means showing how the main points of the essay add up to an **explanation**, **opinion**, **judgement** or **proof**; showing that they add up to more than the sum of the parts.

Example

That previously quoted student's workmanlike essay on education ends:

> More immediately, education is vocational, to help students to pass exams and to prepare for careers that will suit their talents and special interests. But I have made the larger purposes the subject of this essay, because if there were no working towards them there would soon not be a world left to have a career in.

You want the conclusion to be memorable, and like the introduction it might need several drafts. Again, a quote, or a quotation or an anecdote might add vividness to an ending, but don't have one of these both at start and finish.

④ FINALISING THE QUESTION

The conclusion should clinch the matter, there should be a satisfying finality about it.

There will be a definite viewpoint: now you know, the reader is told, why I began as I did. There is a kind of echo to the beginning. There may be a final answer to a question raised at the beginning, or some kind of solution to a problem raised there. Joan Didion, the American writer, brings the rhythms and resonance of poetry into the satisfying conclusion to her essay 'On Morality' (quoted in Thomas S. Kane's *The New Oxford Guide to Writing*):

Because when we start deceiving ourselves into thinking not that we want something or need something, not that it is a pragmatic necessity for us to have it, but that it is a *moral imperative* that we have it, that is when we join the fashionable madmen, and then is when the thin whine of hysteria is heard in the land, and then is when we are in bad trouble. And I think we are already there.

An extra long sentence or an extra short one, or one followed by the other as here, makes for a strong ending.

A **fake conclusion** is easily recognised. Essay writers sometimes try to suggest in their conclusions that they have presented a reasonable argument, or have provided clinching evidence, hoping that some stylish writing will cover up the inadequacy of their attempts. **But it won't**.

⑤ LEAVING SOMETHING TO THINK ABOUT

When the conclusion is tentative, it may appear in the form of a question or an implied judgement, rather than a restatement of a thesis. Joan Didion's 'I think' in the above example shows how to follow conviction with speculation about the future.

In any case, if dealing with an ongoing problem you may want to build up to a new perspective on the topic, give the reader a new question to think about, that will need to draw on the evidence or argument you have provided.

MAKING WHAT MATTERS WORK FOR YOU

✓ Give your own introduction for the essay 'How, do you think, should education prepare us for life?'

● Find a different quotation, or anecdote, to get you started.

● Then write a brief outline for the body.

● Then write a conclusion, including in it a look into the future.

● Get some feedback.

5 Putting the Middle Together

*You know where you started from
and you know your destination.
Choose the best route.*

5 things that really matter

1 **KEEPING TO THE POINT**

2 **NARRATING IN READABLE ORDER**

3 **DESCRIBING PRECISELY**

4 **EXPLAINING FULLY**

5 **ARGUING PERSUASIVELY**

Your finished essay must:

- flow, unified and coherent, with one controlling idea and with points logically connected

- reveal a strong desire to communicate, to share your interest in the topic with your readers.

Getting bogged down in notes or following a plan too rigidly can deaden your interest and weaken your desire to communicate. Conversely, an irritating, shapeless essay can result from neglecting to order. **Experiment with different methods of writing up** to see which works best for you.

It is usually best to concentrate on being **interesting** (sometimes passionate) in your first draft. Leave the final points of style until the second.

Tear up false starts, rewrite plans that don't work and start again. You can refer back to the plan or the notes to see if anything important has been left out.

IS THIS YOU?

In my plans, and even in my first drafts, I tend to have one thing after another without connection. Sometimes it's because I have too many ideas and I haven't decided exactly what they add up to, what the unifying theme is. For example, in an essay entitled 'If I were Prime Minister' I tried to cover so many aspects of life today that it became just a catalogue of ideas.

Having been criticised for this several times, I now tend to sprinkle my final version with faked connectives – 'therefore', 'however', and such phrases as 'on the other hand' and 'having said that . . .' which don't fit the bill.

KEEPING TO THE POINT

To repeat: **keep the topic in front of you at all stages**, at the head of your notes, of your plan, your drafts, even on a card pinned up in front of your desk. It is good to collect too many ideas, as long as you then reduce them to a manageable number that relate directly to the theme.

Be as simple and direct as the subject allows.

Because the way your thoughts are connected is clearer to you than the reader you may fail to supply enough **connectives**. It is a failure of leadership: you must **guide your readers** through a journey that you have just made on your own, and you must anticipate what kind of guidance they need.

Techniques for connecting well are:

● Using conjunctions and conjunctival phrases: and, but, however, so, for example . . . Go easy on the 'ands' and 'buts'.

- **Using key terms.** In the charities article outlined on page 62, key terms (and synonyms and near-synonyms of these) would make a network through the article and might include: charity, good causes, benefits, Lottery, largesse, grants, funds, schemes, scams, money, sponsorship, contributions, distributors, bureaucratic waste, corruption, morality, materialism, collectors, recipients, deserving, undeserving, disadvantaged . . .

- **Signposting.** You link up by referring to statements already made. In effect, you are saying: the foregoing has covered *that*, the following will cover *this*. Simple signposting uses pronouns, demonstratives, definite article and comparative words (he, she, it, this, that, those, the, similar, bigger . . .). Heavier signposting is sometimes needed when a new paragraph changes gear.

- **Summarising link.** You summarise the topic of the last paragraph and then, in the main clause, state the new topic. Take, for example section I, 4 of the charities essay. That could be a paragraph beginning: 'To set against this asessment of the Lottery's contribution [point 3], let's analyse the pros and cons in general of the way charities operate [point 4 introduced].'

- **Parallelism.** Within a paragraph, and from paragraph to paragraph, parellelism makes the structure clear, helping the reader to anticipate what's coming next. Here are some phrases that might steer the reader smoothly through a paragraph or (if the scope is larger) from one paragraph to the next: 'Charities in Elizabethan times . . . Victorian times . . . before the Lottery . . . since the Lottery . . .'

NARRATING IN READABLE ORDER

In an essay you are generally **narrating facts** as well as events. An essay is unlikely to be pure narration, but parts of a literature or history essay may have to concentrate on telling the story. The narration may be mingled with **exposition** (analysing and explaining), or that might follow the charting of events.

Narrative technique depends on choosing the most effective order for the purpose.

- **Chronological order**, suggests itself for simple narration of events, although you may want to vary it by plunging into the story at a dramatic point to grab the reader's interest, filling in the earlier part later. This borrowing of techniques from fiction is common in feature articles but must be done sparingly in essays.

- **Climax order**, the storyteller's main trick, keeps the reader in suspenseful interest (what happened next?) and can be used in essays when appropriate. There, however, the drama is likely to be modified into least important to most important, or unfamiliar to familiar.

- Clarity often demands the **anti-climax order**, from the familiar to the unfamiliar.

Note when the instructional word in a narration topic implies exposition or argument. For example, 'Trace the development of Jane Eyre during Charlotte Bronte's novel' requires a chronological account of her story from childhood to mature woman, but with the significant events identified, their effects on her character explained, plus some interpretation of the author's purpose and methods.

DESCRIBING PRECISELY

The instructional word **describe** is used in two rather different senses:

- paint a word picture of

- give a detailed account of, discuss.

Responding to the instruction in its first sense, as in 'Describe the street you live in as precisely as you can so that the reader would recognise it if they saw it', your aim would be to make readers **see** the street (and perhaps to invoke the other senses as well). The aim is to make readers **feel they are there**.

'Describe the procedures of a typical GPs' practice' has the instruction in the second sense. Your aim would be to help readers understand a logical sequence of events and some explanation of the way the business is managed. If a lengthy essay requiring much discussion is wanted, the instruction may be **describe and explain**.

The two tasks are more difficult to do well than that little word 'describe' suggests. They both need you to use **powers of observation and imagination**!

- Develop your **powers of observation** by going for a walk, keeping your eyes open, writing about what you saw on your return, and later checking to see what you missed.

- Develop your **imagination** by reading the best literature and enlivening your responses to it and to your experiences.

The first topic reminds us that the crucial quality in good writing is **precision** (more about that in Chapter 6). Not only precise words, but **words in the right order** are demanded.

That means the best order for the purpose. In descriptions the best order may be chronological, as in 'Describe a landscape from a moving train'. The best order may be space order, as in describing a town with 'to the north. . . to the south. . . in the middle. . .' Or it may be a combination of these orders.

 EXPLAINING FULLY

To explain, the dictionary tells us, means 'to make something clear by describing it in more detail' or 'give a reason or justification for'. Note the shades of meaning between the various synonyms and near-synonyms used as instructional words: analyse, define, clarify, compare, contrast, assess. Use a dictionary to help you interpret an instructional word.

The essay that explains is called an **exposition**. The basic job is **analyse**: these are its different parts or concepts and this is what they add up to. Such an essay as 'Explain how Parliament works' requires you first to say there are two Houses of Parliament, the Commons and the Lords, who become members and how, and what their duties are. Then, to avoid being buried in abstractions, you look for figures to illustrate points, examples of Parliament at work, anecdotes and analogies (extended comparisons) so that the reader can picture it.

Readers must feel that you are authoritative, the exposition must be knowledgeable and accurate.

If one error is spotted readers will not be able to trust the truth of anything else you say. On a simple level, explaining how to cook chips could result in a house on fire if an important instruction is omitted.

ARGUING PERSUASIVELY

As with an exposition, you generally have to **prepare the ground by analysis** before setting out an argument. For example, you will probably have to **define terms, clarify issues**, or **remove misconceptions**, or all three. Tackling the topic 'Should corporal punishment be banned in schools?' will require fixing where you take corporal punishment to begin, at a gentle slap or at a hard one? You might want to distinguish between primary and secondary schools, and you might want to allow some punishment in one but not in the other.

There are three essential qualities in sound argument:

1. **Clear reasoning**, using such techniques as induction – from the particular to the general, deduction – from the general to the particular, and avoiding fallacies.

2. **Cool weighing of the evidence** of facts and opinions.

3. **Well-considered conclusions**, clearly based on the evidence.

Remember, though, that as the French philosopher Pascal said, the heart has its reasons which reason knows nothing of. Essays on social problems justifiably use emotion to engage readers' sympathy and attention. For essays in the '-ologies' your head will rule more strictly.

MAKING WHAT MATTERS WORK FOR YOU

Comment on the following common flaws in argument, showing where the flaw lies:

✓ **False syllogism.** She told her sister some time ago that if her husband gave up his job she would leave him. She did leave him. So her husband must have given up his job.

✓ **Begging the question.** It is quite obvious that the use of cctv in the streets will reduce the number of robberies.

✓ **Bias, or sweeping generalisation.** Clearly most of the promises the Liberal democrats are making are aimed at doing well at the next General Election.

✓ **Emotionally weighted language.** Young people today, I am told, are more honest, less hypocritical than they used to be. I call them irresponsible and bad mannered, and incapable of carrying on a joined-up conversation because their brains have been rotted by over-exposure to television. They are rarely given the guidance and good example they need from their parents so the parents must share the blame.

6 Writing and Rewriting

When the reader's task is agreeable, you can assume the writer has taken pains.

5 things that really matter

1 **BUILDING STRONG PARAGRAPHS**

2 **ACHIEVING SENTENCE POWER**

3 **DISCOVERING THE RIGHT WORDS**

4 **MATCHING STYLE TO CONTENT**

5 **LEARNING FROM CRITICISM**

When you have studied the topic, thought about it and put your ideas in order, **then is the time to start writing**. Your **writing style** will develop naturally out of what you want to say: it is not something you add on. The style will vary according to the complexity of the subject matter, but it will remain *your* style.

Books cannot teach you how to write. An Army training manual expresses concisely how to learn a skill:

Tell me and I shall forget, show me and I shall remember, let me do it and I shall understand.

You must learn by writing, editing and rewriting, and by trying to write better next time. This book's aim is to guide you to the best strategy for you.

IS THIS YOU?

I am quite good at researching and making notes, I have plenty of ideas and I can plan an essay well. But when it comes to writing it up I easily get stuck. First of all, I find it difficult to make a paragraph hang together – it tends to say one thing after another without showing how they add up. I can't seem to find the right linking words and phrases.

Secondly, my paragraphs and sentences tend to be too long because I can't find the precise words I want. I use too many clichés and sometimes mix metaphors. My tutor laughed loudly when I wrote: 'I always jump over a bridge that a lot of water has passed under' – but it didn't help my grade.

 BUILDING STRONG PARAGRAPHS

Overlong and disjointed paragraphs and sentences, and a reliance on clichés, betray a lack of word power. **It is word power that is the key to writing well.** Words breed thoughts, and thoughts breed words: it's an interactive process. The greater your vocabulary the more likely you are to do more thinking and to think better and more clearly; the more likely you are to **make the right connections**, essential for strong paragraphs. Those connections were illustrated in the 'keeping to the point' section of Chapter 5.

 ACHIEVING SENTENCE POWER

Let's focus more closely on that basic principle, **as simple and as direct as possible**. Here are seven principles that will keep you on the right track:

1. **Average 15 to 20 words a sentence.** Some can be much shorter, a few can be much longer. Try to keep

most sentences to one main point only, and to one subsidiary point.

2. **Vary the lengths, structures, rhythms and emphases of your sentences.** A succession of sentences, which have one main clause and one subordinate clause, produces monotony. Especially when, like that one, they include the lazy 'which'. Vary that construction with prepositional phrases ('with one. . .'), participial phrases ('having one. . .', 'containing. . .').

Just as in paragraphs, the most important words in a sentence are put first or last. Note how you can change the emphasis by changing the order. Consider these examples of rewriting, starting with the most common order of subject, verb, predicate:

(a) Excessive alcohol and lack of exercise can in a short period damage your memory and ability to focus on a subject.

(b) Damage to your memory and ability to focus on a subject: the penalties can quickly follow excessive alcohol and lack of exercise.

(c) The penalties for excessive alcohol . . . are a speedy damage to your memory . . . subject.

(d) It is damage to your memory and ability . . . that can quickly result from . . .

(e) Not only . . . but also . . .

(f) In a short period . . .

Practise doing this with your own sentences.

3. **Use active verbs rather than nouns or passive verbs.**
   'This post **involves a combination of** administration and work in the field' is better expressed as 'This post **combines** . . .'

   The first sentence is gobbledygook, which means using overcomplicated language, and is a common fault in bureaucratic organisations. Gobbledygook also makes excessive use of passive verbs and (worse) impersonal passives.
   Example: 'A decision has been made to . . .' (passive). Rewrite as: 'We have decided . . .'
   Example: 'It is proposed that the replacement of the language courses will be carried out with some degree of urgency' (impersonal passive). Rewrite as: 'We intend to replace the language courses soon.'

4. **Give the result rather than the process. Example**: 'He tried and tried and tried again, using different methods at different times until he finally succeeded.' Rewrite as: 'He finally succeeded.'

5. **Be positive rather than negative. Example**: 'Don't use gobbledygook.' Rewrite as: 'Use plain English.'

6. **Keep related words together. Example**: 'There were a leisure centre and a cinema attracting many people from afar quite near the city centre.' Rewrite as: 'There were a leisure centre and a cinema quite near the city centre attracting many people from afar.'

 DISCOVERING THE RIGHT WORDS

The right word is the **precise** word. That adjective contains the other essentials: conciseness, clarity, appropriateness. Increase your word power by building up your active vocabulary: read, use a good dictionary and thesaurus, and put that increased vocabulary to use. You will find the right words will come more often.

Whenever possible, use:

- short and familiar words rather than long and unfamiliar

- concrete words rather than abstract

- fresh words rather than stale.

Notice how the best writers, with all their differences, obey these principles. The best speeches provide good models too, of how to be instantly comprehensible, as do the pictures simply and vividly painted of Christ's parables in the Bible:

> Consider the ravens, for they sow not, neither do they reap, neither have they storehouse nor barn, and God feedeth them. How much are you more valuable than they?

An economics essay off its guard might say the same thing to much less effect:

> The excessive preoccupation with the accumulation of wealth betrays a reluctance in mankind to deposit the same amount of trust in Providence as is deposited by birds. Human beings should be appreciative of the fact that birds are provided with the necessities of life despite the fact that they show no such preoccupation.

 MATCHING STYLE TO CONTENT

The academic essay at tertiary level has a tone of voice and choice of language more serious, more impersonal than the essays required in earlier years. That **impersonal passive** frowned at above will be needed from time to time. Guidance about such matters is given by good dictionaries, which indicate what they call **register**: telling you that particular words are formal, or informal, or slang, or old-fashioned, or obsolete. They may also give guidance on usage, pointing out that certain terms are offensive, and distinguishing between words often confused, such as **appraise** and **apprise**.

 LEARNING FROM CRITICISM

What you learn from the tutor's corrections and critical notes on your essay usually has to benefit your *next* essay. If you follow the guidance each time you should not fail to improve. That guidance is quite different from the general advice given to all before you embarked on the project. It is personal, specific, directly aimed at your weaknesses, and you can appreciate it fully because of the intellectual journey you have made.

Your tutor's criticism is intended to train you to become your own editor.

Editing may go on as you write, especially if you use a word processor. For convenience let's assume the main editing is done between first and second drafts (preferably after some feedback from fellow-student, or tutor if that's the system). **Leave the first draft for a few days if possible so that you see it with fresh eyes.**

Then edit cautiously, using a pencil and eraser in case you have second and third thoughts. Read through the essay three times to check content and flow, structure and style.

MAKING WHAT MATTERS WORK FOR YOU

Here is a guide to the editing process:

✓ **Content and flow**

Check the length and add or subtract to the content as necessary.

Check that all parts of the essay – paragraphs, sentences, words – are *relevant* to the topic.

Check that all main points made are backed up by *evidence* (eg facts, examples).

Check that sources are acknowledged.

Insert links if necessary to improve the flow.

✓ **Structure**

Check that the title, introduction and conclusion make a good team.

Check with the plan and re-do it if necessary before writing a new draft.

Check that the points made by paragraphs follow a logical pattern. Then check with the plan and decide whether to adjust the essay to the plan or replan.

✓ **Style**

Underline words that need changing.

Underline sentences that need improving. There may be a need for more vigour and more variety, and there may be emphases in the wrong places.

Check that tone of voice and register are consistent.

Check spelling, grammar, usage.

7 Passing the Essay Exam

Writing essays well in exams is a special technique.
Prepare by writing essays under exam conditions.

3

**things that
really matter**

1 **EARNING CONFIDENCE**

2 **ADOPTING WINNING TACTICS**

3 **SPENDING TIME ON REVIEW**

Clearly the expectations of an exam essay are not those of a term essay, even when research sources and notes may be brought in.

Exam essays must be written **at speed** and the polish possible in term essays with precise details of all sources isn't looked for. Nevertheless, you must deal with the topic **as comprehensively as time permits**, showing that you have absorbed the knowledge covered by the course and that you have applied that knowledge with some originality. **Presentation** must be clear, and handwriting legible.

These considerations need not be daunting **if you have prepared well**. Make sure you know what ground the exam is to cover, by consulting a course outline in a handbook or as supplied by a tutor.

Check that the format of the exam will not differ from that of past papers. Resolve any doubts by talking to your tutor.

IS THIS YOU?

My poor showing in exam essays doesn't reflect my ability. I do much better in term essays. I have that sort of temperament. I like to get absorbed in a subject slowly and take twice as long as my fellow-students preparing for a term essay. I read around the topic, becoming fascinated by peripheral issues and taking too many notes, but in the end I'm rewarded by high grades. Unfortunately I don't seem to be able to change gear for the exam essay. I become nervous, and keep looking at my watch. I tend to panic and get confused. All my essay exams are submitted with one or more topics unfinished.

 ## EARNING CONFIDENCE

Many students don't do justice to themselves at exams because they haven't developed the **special technique** required. That is like expecting to know how to ride a bike because you know how to walk. Here is a revision method that will prepare you to be confident at exams:

- **Learn at least as much of the subject as the exam will cover**, and some more.

- **Check it by testing**, orally or in writing, referring afterwards to notes and texts.

- **Apply your knowledge** in a mock exam.

   Learn it. First read through your notes to make sure they are complete. Sources (texts and page numbers) should be indicated clearly. Check against texts any notes that you don't follow, or that appear to be inaccurately taken down.

   Study past exam papers. Would your notes have covered the ground? Do further reading to fill any gaps. Highlight main points if your notes are not on cards.

Check it. Make sure you know what ground is to be covered in the exam, and check that the format will follow that of past papers. Ask a fellow-student to question you on your notes and texts, or put them away and write out main points. Then check.

Read through materials again to fill in any gaps in your knowledge. Check again.

Apply it. Make plans for topics of past papers. Then for practice complete one or two past papers under exam conditions: use notes for this only if they will be allowed at the exam. Then check against notes and texts to see how well you have done.

If mock exams are arranged for you they may be sufficient practice. Check with your tutor.

ADOPTING WINNING TACTICS

Here is some general advice, which you must adapt to your own subject, needs and temperament:

- **Choosing and timing.** First read through all topics and instructions. Allocate a separate sheet for plans and rough work. Submit this with your paper at the end or, if you have time, transfer neatly any plans that might boost your grade if you haven't completed the writing up.

  Decide how much time you will allow for each topic, and/or for planning and for revising at the end.

- **Quickly planning** the essay or essays. The advantage of planning more than one essay at the beginning is that if you run out of time at the end you can quickly flesh out a plan for the last topic. In the last resort you can submit the plan: you'll get some marks for it and it may give a good idea of your grasp of the topic.

A mind map may work well at an exam, or make a simple list of points or questions and indicate the order in which you will deal with them. Indicate in a plan at least one or two links and the conclusion: they make it easier to keep on track when you have to write quickly.

- **Thinking and writing quickly.** If you have prepared well and have learned to perform well at practice exams you will have a bedrock of confidence at the real exam. You will have earned it. Of course you will feel nervous – everybody does. In fact, a little nervousness is good for you on such occasions: it gets the adrenalin flowing, sharpens the mind, and enables you to think and write more quickly than usual.

  Remember that the examiner will be looking for substance rather than elegance. Keep calm. If you find yourself tense, relax your muscles and take a few deep breaths. Do this several times during the exam.

If you go over the time you've allowed yourself for a topic and have still not completed it, **begin a new paragraph** so that you will be able to continue quickly when you return to it. Go on to the next topic. You will get more marks for two nearly completed topics than for one well done, completed topic plus one quite inadequate attempt. Towards the end, complete any essays in notes or plan form (or attach plans already done). But still leave time for review.

 SPENDING TIME ON REVIEW

Ten minutes of editing at the end can make a significant difference to the grade. (Use the editing guide on page 53.)

MAKING WHAT MATTERS WORK FOR YOU

✓ Discover by experiment what sort of study and planning methods described in this book will improve your exam performance.

✓ Don't cram your head with knowledge up to the last minute.

✓ Devise a timetable so that you fit in plenty of preparation study, testing and practice – before the exam.

Appendix A
Responses

Chapter 1

Suggestions only. Yours might be better than mine.

1. (a) 'My favourite restaurant'. Describe your favourite restaurant so that the place comes alive, showing why you prefer it to others.

   (b) 'If I were Prime Minister'. Explain what improvements you would make to the running of the country, concentrating on two or three areas: for example, health, education, crime, drugs, transport.

   (c) 'Friendship'. What do you think is the essential quality of friendship? Illustrate by reference to your own experience.

2. What are the arguments against caring for the mentally ill in the community?

3. (a) Wisdom is **wasted** on the **old**.

   (b) Why were Allied Forces able to make **rapid progress** in their North African **campaigns** of 1942–3 but **slow** to make **progress** in their Italian campaigns of 1943–5?

   (c) Does the increasing **popularity** of **fringe religious groups** indicate that **secularisation** is a **myth**? (A-level Sociology, May 1993, Oxford.)

4. (a) Give the arguments for and against the proposition that by the time we have acquired the knowledge and experience to live sensibly and fruitfully, physical and mental decline prevents us from making the most of that knowledge and experience. (When dealing with such a generalisation for a topic, you need to define key terms carefully. The implied instructional word is 'discuss'.)

   (b) Explain why the Allied Forces' military operation in North Africa in 1942–3 achieved their objectives more quickly than did their operations in Italy, 1943–5 (GCSE Modern World History, June 1993 ULEAC.)

(c)   Argue for or against the proposition that (or how far do you agree that) the popularity of such groups as the Moonies indicates that the secularisation of society has been greatly exaggerated?

Chapter 2

1. Organic food has suddenly become big business, led by supermarkets and high street traders. (14 words)
2. UK farmers and growers, currently meeting 30 per cent of the demand, are converting land for organic produce. (18 words)

Chapter 3

What may be the effects of an increase in leisure time? A question-per-paragraph plan might include the following:

- What effects on individual psychology?

- What effects on family life?

- How would educational objectives change?

- What would be the effects on leisure businesses and ancillary businesses (sports clothing, etc)?

- What new businesses would grow to meet new demands?

- Would more leisure mean more crime or less?

- Which social problems would be more likely to increase?

- Would the overall effects on society be beneficial?

Chapter 5

False syllogism
There are many other reasons why she might have left him and her husband may still be in his job.

Begging the question
CCTV may well reduce street robberies, though even that is not certain. The robbers might discover a way of rendering them inoperative, giving the authorities a false sense of security, and that could bring about an increase. In any case, even if cctv did reduce robberies in the street, more robberies might be carried out away from streets.

Bias, or sweeping generalisation
Superlatives (eg, 'most'), and words like 'clearly', should be avoided in argument unless well supported by facts. There is *some* truth in the argument, which can no doubt be supported by facts, but some does not mean the whole truth.

Emotionally weighted language
There is probably a lack of facts to support the strong belief (or prejudice) here. This is rationalising (supporting a belief on irrational grounds), bolstered by emotional language.

Appendix B
Formal Outline

SHOULD CHARITY BE LEFT TO THE STATE?

Introduction

1. Anecdote as hook
2. Define 'charity' and 'charity organisation'. As examples: list main charities and indicate work of one or two. The picture has changed since start of Lottery.
3. The argument about current role of the State, and the effect of the receiving of Lottery funds. Argument for rationalising by much more centralising control.
4. Viewpoint: Answer to question is no. More government control desirable, but without losing benefits of individual efforts. *First the need to describe how the partnership works.*

I   The way charity works

1. The government role in general: controls, central distribution. *Within this, role of Lottery.*
2. The Lottery and good causes: 25p out of every pound to 'good causes' via five organisations including the arts, sports, etc and Charities Board: give figures. Great benefits overall, but discourages direct giving of both government and individuals.
3. Gains by some charities, losses by others (interviews, figures). *Also:*
4. Pros and cons of the way charities work: inspired voluntary efforts; but danger of scams and embezzlements. *Taking these aspects one by one.*

II   Control and bureaucracy

1. Advantages of more centralised control: eg, prevention of scams. *But two main disadvantages:*

2. (a)   How more centralised government control might produce more bureaucratic waste. *Whereas*:
   (b)   Charities easier to organise locally, can identify local needs quickly.
3. Suggestions for getting the best of both worlds. *What is clear from above is that:*

III More regulation needed

1. Brief history of charities: attempts to regulate.
2. Current waste of funds on administration.
3. Scams can be hard to detect.

The role of the Lottery needs special attention:

IV The Lottery connection: suggested improvements

1. Contrast government, business and charities' views on how Lottery affects charities.
2. Their suggestions for improvements to the system.
3. Suggestions compared with press commentaries.
4. Sum up viewpoint on this aspect.

What must not be lost sight of is:

V   The philosophical and psychological arguments

1. The State cannot legislate for morality.
2. 'Charity begins at home': implications for morality.
3. The dangers of encouraging materialism.

VI Conclusion

1. Sum up reforms needed.
2. Anecdote, quote or example showing a charity working at its best.